Way of the White Dragon

Pai Lum Tao
Way of the White Dragon

Glenn C. Wilson

UP UNIQUE PUBLICATIONS
Burbank, California

Disclaimer

Please note that the author and publisher of this book are NOT RESPONSIBLE in any manner whatsoever for any injury that may result from practicing the techniques and/or following the instructions given within. Since the physical activities described herein may be too strenuous in nature for some readers to engage in safely, it is essential that a physician be consulted prior to training.

First published in 2000 by Unique Publications.

Library of Congress Catalog Number:
ISBN: 0-86568-179-1

Unique Publications
4201 Vanowen Place
Burbank, CA 91505
(800) 332–3330

First edition
05 04 03 02 01 00 99 98 97 1 3 5 7 9 10 8 6 4 2

Printed in the United States of America

DEDICATION

The premier printing of the Pai Lum Tao System
is dedicated to my mother, Jean, and the four men
who helped raise me—my biological father, Charles R. Wilson;
my stepfather, Tom Latimore; my uncle, Ross Wilson;
and my teacher, Daniel Kane Pai.
I will be forever grateful.

I would like to make a special dedication to my family,
who remain the most important thing in the world to me.
They include my wife, Hilda Guererro Wilson,
my four boys, Richie, Charlie, Levi and Lance Wilson,
and my grandson, Brandon Wilson.

Also, in loving memory of Dr.
Daniel Kane Pai and his love,
Simo—Denise Vigi.

INFORMATION

Information offered in this book has come from a variety of sources. Some was taught to me by my teacher, Dr. Daniel Kane Pai, in person as well as through the manuals and tapes he gave me for study purposes.

If any information, or its lack thereof, in this book offends anyone it is purely coincidental. I wish my brothers and sisters in Pai Lum Tao the very best and hope they continue to progress in their studies.

"In the spirit of the White Dragon"
Si Tai Gung—Glenn C. Wilson

ACKNOWLEDGEMENTS

I would like to give special thanks to the following people for their help and guidance: Michelle Cady, Tricia Kyzar, Jeff Sindy, Robert Murphy, Ron Caimano, Bob Earl, Mack McPhail, and to the photographers, Jaimee Itagaki and Don Corless.

Special thanks also go out to Cynthia Rothrock and Don "The Dragon" Wilson.

My wife, Hilda, and son, Lance, who have been so patient with my time. And all the members of the White Dragon Warrior Society, Inc.

CONTENTS

PREFACE
Pai Lum Tao—"A Way of Life"

The spirit of an art is found within its execution of motion. To know the spirit of Pai Lum Tao is to master its way. This "way", the "way" we train, has been called Pai Lum, Pai Lum Tao, Bai Lung, Pai Te Lung, Pai Te Lung Chuan Shih Yang, White Lotus, Bok Leen Pai, Pai Yung Tai Chi Chuan, Kuan Yin Chi Kung, White Dragon, Fire Dragon, White Fire Dragon, and Pai Lung Kuen Po. We constitute the Gong Yuen Chuan Fa Pai Pao Lung Gar family of the teachings of Great Grandmaster, SiJo Dr. Daniel Kane Pai.

Pai Lum Tao teaches you how to balance energy in all realms of life. This balance helps us understand that the mind, body and spirit are a perfect blend for martial arts as well as life. The mind is expanded with tranquil meditation exercises as well as with the harmonious movements of the Kuan Yin Chi Kung. The body is stretched, strengthened and chiseled to meet the challenge of the rigorous routines of the Dragon Way. The spirit is enriched by the studies of the in-depth philosophies, creeds, codes and formulas for health and wholeness.

That's right, Pai Lum Tao—Way of the White Dragon, is not just a way to throw a punch or a kick, a way to throw or lock an opponent into submission. It is a *way of life*.

Practicing the Pai Lum Tao way will strengthen the spirit of the practitioner as well as shine a light on one's middle path to harmony and peace. The balance of Yin and Yang is the very core of traditional Pai Lum Tao. The practitioner learns to adjust or evade obstacles in his kung-fu technique and his daily challenges.

As a fighting system it is second to none. Time-tested theories and formulas have allowed the system to not only survive, but also to flourish in an era where challenge can be found around every corner. This powerful system has developed champions and legends such as Great Grandmaster Daniel Kane Pai, Don "The Dragon" Wilson, Rusty Gray, James Wilson, Cynthia Rothrock, Mike Crane, Gino Carrello, Fred Schmidts, Dave Everett, Jim Cravens, and, of course, Grandmaster Glenn C. Wilson. Pai Lum Tao builds champions in life as well as in the martial arts.

Once again we see the balance.

Simo—Hilda Guerrero Wilson
Black—4th Higher Level

Great Grandmaster Dr. Daniel Kane Pai
Pai Lao Lung

Pai Lum Tao—"A Way of Life"
Great Grandmaster—Pai Lum Tao
Pai Te Lung Chuan Kung-Fu
Bok Leen Pai Kenpo
Pai Yung Tai Chi
Kuan Yin Chi Kung
Chin Kon Pai Meditation

Daniel Kane Pai was born April 30, 1930, in Kameula, HI. He lived the last 17 years of his life in Florida and died in 1993 in the Dominican Republic. Per his request, he was laid to rest in his beloved Hawaii. During his 63-year journey on earth, he built one of the greatest and most-respected martial arts legacies in North America. While Dr. Pai is gone, his memory and system live on through a few, hand-picked Sigung and several Sifu who carry the teachings of the "Way of the White Dragon."

Although considered a controversial figure in martial arts, he also was universally respected for his unswerving devotion to a high set of personal and professional ideals. Daniel Kane Pai always did it his way, whether it was surviving on the tough streets of Hawaii or forming the largest kung-fu system in North America during the 1960s–70s. He was Pai Lum and Pai Lum was he. He taught a rough-tough style of martial arts for which the Hawaiian Islands became famous.

A young Daniel began his formal martial arts training with family members in Hawaii in the disciplines of kung-fu, kenpo and judo-jiu-jitsu. In the 1940s his grandfather, Pai Po Fong, taught him the "Pai Family" martial arts, which predominantly contained elements of Dragon, Crane and Tiger. Once he mastered the Tiger forms, the Dragon, Crane, Leopard and Snake forms were introduced to the young practitioner.

During his early years of training, Pai Po Fong sent Daniel to study and learn stern discipline from the teachers of the White Lotus Monastery "Byakurenji" on the north coast of Okinawa. He hoped that learning the ways of the monks would settle young Daniel down and provide a base in which to develop his life and art. Daniel loved the rigorous training, the monks' devotion to a single, solitary purpose. He began to grow—physically, mentally and spiritually. In the early 1950s, Daniel began to merge his knowledge of martial arts and philosophy into what would later become known as Pai Lum Tao —"Way of the White Dragon". He took his newfound system to the U.S. mainland.

Daniel was as much a student as he was a teacher—eager to master and eager to learn. He was a teacher of martial arts, a graduate with a doctorate from the Chicago Medical College, a bodyguard, stunt coordinator, cowboy at the Parker Ranch with the late Ed Parker, philosopher, biker and decorated Korean War veteran. In the 1970s, Dr. Pai formed the U.S. White Dragon Martial Arts Society to begin the process of standardizing his vast knowledge of martial arts. The students of the 1960–70s who weathered Pai's rigorous and, at times, brutal training became known as the "old school" lineage.

Dr. Pai's American team was awarded the Superb Achievement Merit at the Kuoshu event in Taipei in 1976. In 1980 Dr. Pai served as director at the 3rd World Chinese Kuoshu tournament in Hawaii. During Dr. Pai's visit to Taipei in 1983, he was appointed the United States Vice President of the worldwide Promotion Association's executive board of the Kuoshu Federation of the Republic of China. As president of the United States Chinese Kuoshu Federation in 1989 he organized the much-talked about World Chinese Kuoshu tournament in Las Vegas, Nev.

In 1990, Dr. Pai and disciple Glenn C. Wilson began work on uniting the different factions of Pai Lum Tao martial arts, as well as standardizing the curriculum and legitimizing rank. The fruits of that labor can be found in the "White Dragon Warrior Society." Chaired by Grandmaster Glenn C. Wilson, the Society is dedicated to keeping alive the dreams of Great Grandmaster Daniel Kane Pai.

"My teacher lived and died by his belief of Pai Lum Tao: ever learning, ever changing." This truly is the Way of Life.

Si Tai Gung Glenn C. Wilson
"Pai Pao Lung Huit"

Grandmaster Glenn C. Wilson
Pai Pao Lung Huit

Grandmaster—Gong Yuen Chuan Fa Pai Pao Lung Gar
Professor—Bok Leen Pai Kenpo
Master—Pai Te Lung Chuan Kung-Fu
Master—Pai Yung Tai Chi
Master—Kuan Yin Chi Kung
Master—Shaolin Chuan Fa—Moi Fah
Chairman of the Board—White Dragon Warrior Society, Inc.
World Champion—Hall of Famer
Disciple of Dr. Daniel Kane Pai

ABOUT THE AUTHOR
Grandmaster—Professor—Glenn C. Wilson

Glenn C. Wilson was born to Native American and European parents in the early 1950s in Orlando, Fla. His father's affiliation with the Air Force gave Glenn his first taste of martial arts.

After living in Spain for many years, the family moved back to the United States, spending time first in Florida, then Texas and back to Florida. Shortly after his 9th birthday, Glenn witnessed a judo demonstration, which would change his life forever. But his father, a judoka, would not let him train until he proved to be more disciplined. On Glenn's 10th birthday he began what would become a lifelong devotion to martial arts. He started in Kodokan Judo and then moved on to the Kwon styles of Korea.

When he was 15 he witnessed a Kenpo demonstration that fascinated him more than anything he'd ever experienced. The smooth, fluid and extremely powerful techniques mystified the young martial artist, who to this day holds a major reverence for its curriculum. Glenn studied the various Kenpo disciplines of Tracy's Kenpo, Shorinji Kempo, Kongo Do Kenpo, Chinese Kenpo and finally a style that would stay with him for life—Bok Leen Pai Kenpo.

He made the natural transition from his Kenpo roots to the various studies of Chuan Fa. Glenn trained in Gong Yuen Chuan Fa, Lo Han Chuan, Moi Fah Chuan, Five Animal methods, White Crane, and—Pai Te Lung Chuan of Pai Lum Tao—a style that captured his imagination and gave new meaning to his martial arts pursuits.

The internal influences that would help him center his life and training were practiced in Pai Lum Tao's systems of Pai Yung Tai Chi, Kuan Yin Chi Kung and Chin Kon Pai Meditation.

Glenn's life would change for good in 1974 when he went from the private outdoor (very secluded) training of Master Jim McIntosh to being accepted as a disciple of martial arts legend Great Grandmaster Dr. Daniel Kane Pai. Glenn was brought into the Pai Lum Tao System at the rank he held at the time—a third higher level. Five years later Dr. Pai elevated Glenn to Master and named him head of his family of Pai Lum Tao martial arts.

Several years before Dr. Pai's passing, he and his disciple, Glenn, formed the White Dragon Warrior Society. The formation was designed to preserve the traditions of Pai Lum Tao, share and strengthen the system and legitimize rank among the families. Dr. Pai served as the Chairman of the Board and Co-Founder, while Glenn was Vice Chairman of the Board of the White Dragon Warrior Society, Inc. (after Dr. Pai's passing Glenn became Chairman of the Board), President of Glenn Wilson's Fire Dragon Academies, Inc., and Head Coach of the Wilson's Warriors Competition/Demonstration Team.

Great Grandmaster Pai died in 1993. This left Grandmaster Glenn C. Wilson in charge of the Society they formed—the White Dragon Warrior Society—as well as Senior Master of his "own" Family of Pai Lum Tao.

Glenn Wilson is considered a grandmaster's grandmaster. He is what a Grandmaster should be: He doesn't talk the game, he lives the life—A Pai Lum Tao Way of Life.

Respectfully
His Pai Lum Tao Student,
Don "The Dragon" Wilson

白龍道
PAI LUM TAO

A Brief History

While much speculation revolves around the history of early China's fighting arts, it is generally believed they were popularized by the monks of Shaolin Ssu. Although history books and popular accounts point to a host of hand-to-hand combative systems existing at that time throughout Asia, few are as well-known or as universally accepted as Shaolin Ssu.

Pai Lum Tao's teachings tell us the Kung-Fu-Chuan Fa-Kenpo practiced by the monks of Shaolin Ssu were not just a martial art, but a way of life held in the highest regard. Daily routines were practiced to unify the energies of body and mind. Monks did not create or practice kung-fu as a means of self-defense, but rather as a form of self-preservation through synchronized exercise routines such as the Shi Pa Lo Han Sho. Kung-fu grew into a balance of physical exercise, spiritual training and time-tested personal protection. Eventually, the practice gained fame as Shaolin Chuan. As weapons use grew throughout China, demand spread for its powerful and far-reaching techniques.

In A.D. 574, the Shaolin Temple was destroyed by the armies of Emperor Wu Ti. When the Temple was rebuilt during the Sui Dynasty (A.D. 589–618) it resulted in the underground practice and spread of Shaolin Chuan throughout China. Kung-fu contin-

1

ued to be tested by practitioners fighting suppression brought on by the Mongol Ming and Manchu Dynasties.

During the Manchu Dynasty, many kung-fu masters fled China to practice their arts in peace. Okinawa became a popular haven. Settling on the northern coast of Okinawa, a group of Chinese refugees built their monastery where they could practice their ancient arts. These early immigrants to the island became known as the monks of White Lotus.

Early in the 20th century, a highly skilled practitioner of Chinese boxing named Pai Po Fong moved from the Singapore region to Hawaii to better provide for his family. He brought with him the Pai family's martial arts systems of Dragon and Crane. Pai Po Fong shared and added to his already-rich system of martial arts after his arrival in Hawaii.

Pai Po Fong sent his highly skilled and spiritual grandson, Daniel, to the White Lotus Monastery in Okinawa to train with monk relatives. Pai Po hoped spending time with the monks would calm his grandson down and give him a sense of purpose.

Daniel Kane Pai's legend grew when he returned to the Hawaiian Islands. His fighting skill was unmatched, his devotion to a life of martial arts universally admired. In 1953 Grandmaster Daniel K. Pai began teaching his awesome style of martial arts on the U.S. mainland. His style gained overnight attention and respect from those who saw it and those who fought against it. He called his method Pai Lum Tao—The Way of the White Dragon.

Pai Lum Tao's fame spread throughout the world, producing many world-class forms, fighting, and weapons champions. Although its practitioners number in the tens of thousands, only a handful of certified masters have been charged with guiding its future. Much is asked of the Pai Lum Tao master. He or she must show respect for the style's tradition and prove worthiness in martial arts technique.

Pai Lum Tao is the perfect art for a new millennium. The organization formed by Daniel Kane Pai and Glenn C. Wilson, the White Dragon Warrior Society, is destined to grow and improve for generations to come.

The Society teaches Honor, Integrity, Courage, Pride and loyalty to self and others.

The "Society" serves as a nucleus to:

- Preserve the traditions of Pai Lum Tao's disciplines: kung-fu-kenpo-tai chi;
- Legitimize and document rank;
- Establish and teach the by-laws; and
- Educate other martial arts systems and the general public to the true values of Pai Lum Tao.

Philosophy

Dragon Code

I am what I am because I chose to be. I am a Dragon by

Choice, and subject to its law. My brothers and sisters are

My heart and my mind. And even though we may disagree

With each other, we still strive to be one. Forgetting all

Categories, and letting energy that wishes to exist, exist.

But as a Dragon, I must go forth to seek the Tao and the void,

Understanding myself and finding peace within.

—SiJo Dr. Daniel Kane Pai

白龍道

龍的格言

我就是我，因定是我的選擇，我選擇做龍，就要遵守這準則，我的弟兄姊妹就是我的心和智。雖然我們間中不委協，但我們仍然團結一致。忘記你有分類，而由原動力去生存，去發揚光大。但由於我是龍，我務必要去尋找那道兩道之間的真絆，明白自我父尋找內裡太平。

Warrior Code

The warrior is a man who dedicates his life to the cause which Made him what he is. What governs the warrior is the foresight that he has to see beyond the present and into the future, beyond the capabilities of those who follow him. The warrior is dedicated to defend the honor, the creed, the pride, and the self-respect for what he wishes to be called . . . dragon, dragon, dragon. Wisdom, courage, honor, strength, purity and all knowledge.

—SiJo Dr. Daniel Kane Pai

I Be

I am because of the nights and days I have seen, I believe I am

A man for the things I have done, but all it is, is just feelings of

Sensations that are created in my mind. Those that I touch know

Me as I am, These simple arts that are called Kung-Fu are the

Feelings I have of the things I now love, these high sensations

And thrills of my spine, are not love but a practitioner's body that

Cares for his art. If I sound as if I am a dreamer, then let me dream

As I practice this martial art that is called Kung-Fu, these strange

Feelings I have of knowing the word called devotion.

—SiJo Dr. Daniel Kane Pai

Standard of Ethics

When you fight, the fear of getting hurt can be found in what you don't understand. Once you can absorb that hurt feeling, everything will become easier.

In the Way of the White Dragon, we learn to read a person—not judge him—but read his innermost thoughts and feelings. We try to see how he will react to you.

Before all else, White Dragon people are honorable, courteous and humble. Being a true White Dragon means not having to tell people who or what you are. They should be able to tell just by watching your actions and listening to your words. Being overly confident is not the Way of the White Dragon. If you are a true White Dragon, you are confident of your skills, so much so you need not let others know how good you can be. Let them make up their own mind and decide if you are what you claim. If you are good don't say it, but be ready to prove it if the need arises.

One of our teachings explains: All of us are equal in flesh and blood, but we are not all equal in our capacity and hunger for learning. The knowledge you have now, no matter how great, is not enough. When we stop learning, we stop growing. White Dragon believes in the exchange of knowledge, not in achieving it and keeping it to oneself. This helps us obtain unity by sharing our knowledge with each other. Then we become as one. One soul, one mind, one body: The White Dragon.

I am what I am because I chose to be.

I am a Dragon by choice and subject to its law.

Fighting Theories (Introduction)

Pai Lum Tao as a way of life teaches us to follow the middle path. The path that one takes may go linear, circular, oval, or up and down. The middle path keeps us centered so we can pursue the flow of the attack. The ancient movements of combat would flow from and to the four directions. Knowing the intent of your attacker will lend to your flow of direction. Within the four directions lies the figure-eight pattern. This merger and cultivation of theories is a time-tested formula for success.

For generations Pai Lum Tao fighters have proven the success of their system in a myriad field of battles—the street, a ring or in a martial arts tournament setting. The teachings of Great Grandmaster Daniel Kane Pai have placed his Pai Lum Tao system among the greatest martial arts fighting systems in history.

Training is not easy, but then nothing rewarding comes without a price. The White Dragon practitioner must train from the ground up. Countless hours of low square horse, bow and arrow, and lunging stances create legs of iron and a solid foundation on which to build. The 5-step square horse is practiced with the synchronization of smooth and powerful blocks and punches. The movements of the White Dragon are smooth, fluid and powerful, moving in the Nei and striking in the Wei.

To move in the Nei is to move with the fluidity of the wind and carry the crashing power of water. The body remains relaxed and executes whipping and cutting techniques. This allows the body to execute maximum speed through articulate timing. Reaction time is lessened when the muscles are in a relaxed nature. Chi Kung exercises accentuate the Nei movements by creating a relaxed, yet powerful nature—the secret behind all Pai Lum Tao strikes. The term "smooth, fluid and power" becomes second nature after thousands of routines are put to the test.

When the saying, "Strike the Wei" is heard, the powerful strikes for which Pai Lum Tao is revered can be felt in all its glory. At the time of impact, the surface of the utensil used to strike tightens and cuts through an unsuspecting target. This fighting theory shows how the energy expelled by the practitioner is concentrated on a smaller area and actually accentuated by the increased explosion. Simple, total relaxation during the delivery maximizes the power at the time of delivery. This fighting theory has been one of the main ingredients behind a long and studded line of successful Pai Lum Tao fighters.

Proper breathing is essential in all Chinese martial arts systems. And the same holds true for Pai Lum Tao. Formal training in Chi Kung offers one way of developing breathing. Practicing and exercising unified breath lies at the core of successful fighting. Timing of the physical technique in conjunction with correct breathing remains the heart of Chi Kung technique. Short- and long-breath training aids in short-range explosive techniques, while providing added staying power to the long-range variety.

Understanding free-form motion is extremely important. One's fighting techniques must be free to move as instincts and reflexes dictate. When challenged, a practitioner must react confidently but naturally. A natural reaction is formed through the practice of techniques aligned with theory. If you must think before you react, that added time may cost you your life.

As is the case with many martial arts, fighters in the Pai Lum Tao system are more likely to use punches than kicks. In fact, the ratio can be as high as 70-percent punching to 30-percent kicking. A well-equipped arsenal of sometimes deceptive, but always explosive hand strikes become the main thrust for a successful encounter.

With minimal movement, motion will close the gap between technique and target. This helps you strike quickly and effectively before your opponent can recover. Explosiveness is vital to success. When you sense your opponent's next move, it is critical to close the gap as quickly and as naturally as possible. This requires a combination of foresight, reaction, displacement and execution. Essentially, a fighter needs the *foresight* to see what may happen; the *reaction* to what is happening, the *displacement* of the assault in a safe direction; and the *execution* of technique to finish the assault.

The premise behind Pai Lum Tao fighting is all about the natural rhythm of movement. The scenario is played in the mind of the practitioner and creates a unity of body and thought process. Thus, the theories weave into a natural balance of stance, body posture, waist whipping, and striking (punch or a kick).

Understanding Pai Lum Tao's fighting theories is about experiencing the relationship between the triumphant warrior and life: the beauty and effectiveness of the art and the polished skill that unleashes this extraordinary ability. The best-skilled fighters of all time understood this natural occurrence.

The nature of fighting teaches us the importance of accuracy, balance and speed. We must master which one to enhance and when. To know:

- When to advance, when to retreat,
- When to stand fast, when to evade,
- When to direct, when to redirect,
- When to strike, when to fake the strike,
- When to expel Chi, when to steal Chi,
- Always understand the value of mercy.

> *"With a single evasion the warrior taught honor,*
> *with a thousand punches he learned disgrace."*
>
> —Si-Tai Gung Glenn C. Wilson

Strategy

"The end result—broken down in stages."

You must train diligently, sharpen the mind and feed the spirit. Once you have acquired these virtues, your plan of action or method is used to gauge power, speed and timing. When these three qualities are in the place, the strategy begins long before the confrontation. It is all about developing perception. Learning to become insightful opens a vast wealth of "learning"; reading the situation in advance will ultimately control the direction of the story.

Strategy leads to the formation of "conscious thought". Persevering and reacting are the keys to conscious thought, which send a message to the "tool" to be utilized in a situation. A barrage of techniques are executed in perfect harmony to the rhythms of the attacker. Now you have taken control of the situation. Strategy is learned and then increased with the accumulation of knowledge. The physical and psychological must be in balance for the practitioner to find "the Way".

The Way is the direct, indirect, circular, linear, hard, soft, rhythm, pattern, execution, ability, experience, and most of all "understanding" of the true White Lotus Way.

Stancework

Stances remain the foundation of all martial arts disciplines. Just as the mightiest oak tree is only as strong as its roots, a firm understanding of the utilization of the stationary and transitory stance philosophy is a must to the most basic Pai Lum Tao practitioner.

The beginner will spend countless hours developing the leg strength that will help him move swiftly and effectively from stance to stance. The practitioner must understand that moving effectively is far more than just a physical task; it begins with the proper mental attitude. Training begins with memorizing one of the 3-step philosophies of Pai Lum Tao: stance, posture, technique. This philosophy ensures strength, efficiency, preparedness and alertness when the moment of truth is presented.

Pai Lum Tao teaches you to reach your potential. This means that stances should be as low and as strong as humanly possible within the guidelines of achieving maximum results. If you can master the square horse stance 12 inches from the ground, fighting when your stance is 24 inches off the ground should be no problem.

When to use a specific stance is as important as what stance to use. Everything you do will be rooted in stance. Two of the most important factors will be angle and distance from the attacker.

Where your attacker is standing in relation to you will dictate the alignment of your stance. It may only be a few inches forward or backward; a few degrees right or left. Consider the dilemma of an archer who may only have to move the draw hand a fraction to change the outcome by a foot. Angles are many; they begin with basic linear and circular movements then use various combinations of footwork to create what is called the Dragon's Maze. This maze represents the intricate footwork patterns practiced in Pai Lum Tao. These complex footwork patterns will confuse, disorientate, and keep the attacker off guard. A properly chosen and executed stance can dislodge the opponent's own stance and put his motion out of harmony. Once he has become dislodged or lost his harmony, he is at the mercy of the Pai Lum Tao movements. As an old Chinese proverb states, "Control the weight of your opponent and you can defeat anyone."

Understanding distance is crucial when deciding an appropriate stance. It is the first line of defense when a confrontation appears imminent. At a long distance you may choose to settle into a lower, more powerful-type stance to assess the situation. This is known as positioning and focusing. In an encounter when the opponent is closer, a higher stance allows for greater mobility and maneuverability. This proves advantageous when following another 3-step philosophy: evade, strike, finish.

The practitioner must take into consideration many factors when choosing a stance, including environment, ground surface, distance of attacker and type of attack (armed or unarmed). Maneuverability also is a prime consideration; if you cannot move, all else fails. Body positioning, when combined with correct weight distribution, gives the practitioner the key elements on which to build his defense.

The beginner student must reach a level of proficiency in his stancework before he can learn Pai Lum Tao's awesome fist sets. The basic stances to be conquered are:

5-Step Square Horse Stance

BOW AND ARROW STANCE

BREAK STANCE

CAT STANCE

COILED SNAKE STANCE

PIGEON STANCE

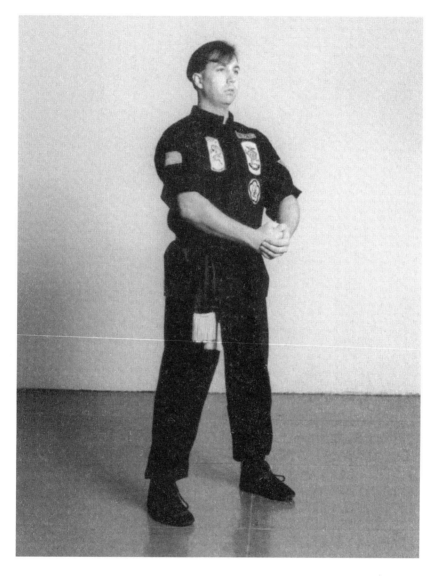

READY STANCE

REVERSE CAT

RISING HORSE

SCISSORS STANCE

SHORT BOW

SIDE HORSE STANCE

STRETCHING TIGER

TWISTING HORSE

These stances are held as long as possible to ensure maximum leg and lower back strength. Stances are also practiced in a low posture to aid in understanding Pai Lum Tao's discipline. The 5-step square horse is practiced in two separate disciplines. First, as low as possible for strength, discipline and as a mental challenge; then high for maneuverability and creativity of motion.

If the student can withstand the demands of the stancework he will have mastered the fundamentals necessary to begin his self-defense fist sets and the basic tiger forms.

"Hours of basic meditating stancework prepare the Pai Lum Tao disciple's body, mind and spirit for any challenge."

—Si Tai Gung Glenn C. Wilson

Blocks (Hard and Soft)

Pai Lum Tao places a great deal of emphasis on the training of blocks. Although this constitutes a large category of training, those who master them will find a greater understanding of the system. Basic blocking theories begin with perpendicular, circular, then force modification techniques. All basic blocks begin with box set zoning. This box area is defended by utilizing Gong Chuan hard fist blocks to the upward, inward, outward and, finally downward zone. The forearms are conditioned through partner training and the application of 7 star training principles. The box set drill is executed while assuming the 5-step square horse stance. Rhythm, timing and speed is the formula for execution. A practitioner must achieve proper blocking with one arm to all four zones within a second before he can advance to the next level of blocking training.

Circular blocking sequences can be done with both Gong (hard) and Yuen (soft) hand techniques. Gong techniques teach crushing the oncoming assault, while Yuen techniques emphasize cutting through the attack. Circular patterns teach the arm to move like a sword slicing through the air. This motion will meet the attacker's normal force and guide it into tangential force. Applying the circular pattern to the thrust of an attack changes direction and power while simultaneously cutting into the initial power. This steals an attacker's thunder and allows the defender to become the person in charge.

A Pai Lum Tao student begins to understand energy and the utilization of an opponent's force when practicing force modification blocks. Principles such as sliding, windmill, evading, constricting and smothering play an intricate role in modifying an attacker's force. These techniques are natural to the flow of the attack and often represent set-ups for takedowns, throws or locks. Understanding the nature of force modification takes proper tutelage and a patient student. Evasive or yielding patterns are preferred over exerting direct force or power against your attacker's forward movement. These sophisticated and intricate maneuvers, regarded as the nucleus of Pai Lum Tao's Chin Na and Shuai Chiao disciplines, become pure poetry in motion to the executioner and a harsh reality to the attacker.

Direction and force are key in the application of a successful block. Direction determines the sequence of counters to be performed. It will make the attacker rotate out of his center and leave him wide open for a counter.

Force will be determined by the distance and positioning of the attacker after the redirection has occurred. With lightning speed, force will then expel in an articulate execution of techniques. Various "power" strikes will offset the attacker's weight distribution and positioning. This will ultimately signal victory for the Pai Lum Tao practitioner.

Try watching the way animals fight, or more specifically, how they block. By understanding your "safety zone" and your "response zone" you learn when response is necessary and when disregarding the attack is in your best interest. Most animals fight only as a last resort. This is a virtue taught to the Pai Lum Tao student from the outset. First and foremost, we are legally and morally responsible for our response. When you reach the point of no return, your response should be executed as fast and as effortless as possible. Because of the intricate, complex and lightning-quick hand techniques of Pai Lum Tao, it is often difficult to see what the practitioner has delivered. But the final result—a beaten attacker—will be right before your eyes.

With such an emphasis on blocking, it is clear that this segment of the Pai Lum Tao curriculum should not be thought of as a separate identity to the counterkick or kick. A basic formula of movement in Pai Lum Tao states that the block *is* the counter, meaning that once motion has started, all movement and energy become the counter. If someone throws a punch, you must eliminate the immediate threat or the punching arm. Your choices include crushing, slicing or modifying force to the attacking arm, then continuing with a barrage of countertechniques to other vital areas. The initial block-strike constitutes the beginning of a counter.

Pai Lum Tao practitioners are trained to anticipate every action so a host of on-guard positions are practiced in conjunction with a variety of blocks. Stances and body posture alignments are the focal point from which the blocks will flow.

"There is no block faster than the illusion created by evasion."

—Si Tai Gung Glenn C. Wilson

INWARD GONG CHUAN

OUTWARD GONG CHUAN

UPWARD GONG CHUAN

DOWNWARD GONG CHUAN

INWARD YUEN CHUAN

OUTWARD YUEN CHUAN

UPWARD YUEN CHUAN

DOWNWARD YUEN CHUAN

**UPWARD CRANE CROSSING WINGS
WITH GONG CHUAN**

DOWNWARD CRANE CROSSING WINGS
WITH GONG CHUAN

**UPWARD CRANE CROSSING WINGS
WITH YUEN CHUAN**

DOWNWARD CRANE CROSSING WINGS
WITH YUEN CHUAN

CRANE'S BEAK

DOUBLE BRUSHING PALM

INWARD CRANE WING SNAPS

MONKEY'S PAW

THUNDERING HAMMERS

TWIN PINES

WINDMILL PALMS

Dr. Daniel Kane Pai teaching his student Professor Glenn C. Wilson
the Secret Trapping Hands of Pai Lum Tao.

Punches

In a fight, the Pai Lum Tao student is taught to envision the motion generated by the opponent's hand or foot. Like a bolt of lightning, the absolute fist is generated and becomes a mirror image of motion. This type of training philosophy has helped create the legend of Pai Lum Tao's lightning punches. Through the continuous training of body-mind unity the White Dragon fist is a respected piece of the practitioner's arsenal.

The practitioner begins with thousands of repetitions of Gong Chuan hand strikes. These punches are delivered in a short-range sequence from a square horse stance, then long range from the twisted horse stance. The basic patterns begin with a ram's head punch then continue with sun fist, back knuckle, hammer fist, reverse hammer fist and upper cut punch. Though the fist is utilized like an iron sledgehammer the arm and body must remain relaxed until contact. The student's first goal is to achieve shallow penetration, work his way to deep penetration and finally master the cut-through punches. The human body has very little resistance to these cutting series of strikes.

The punches open with linear and circular patterns, followed immediately by the arm rapidly snapping back in preparation for another strike. Next comes a rapid-fire barrage of punches to various weak points of the body. Even though the first punch has done its job, one of the distinct characteristics of Pai Lum Tao is to not leave anything to chance.

Since Pai Lum Tao teaches hard and soft as well as external and internal theories, conditioning of the hands is a natural process. Conditioning is done slowly and safely. The progression of training will be one of well-deserved confidence. The student begins with the soft bag and drills the hard bag, padded wood, rope pole, split wooden dummy and finally, if he has shown dedication, the Iron Dummy. This proven ladder of success will take years under the watchful eyes of a legitimate Pai Lum Tao sifu.

Mastering the fist series of exercises is essential to understanding the teachings of the Dragon. The student learns to chamber at the waist (not the hip). Energy from the punch will originate at the root, is regenerated by waist whipping and finally expelled as part of the striking weapon. This is better known as dragon whipping.

The concept of energy flow must be understood before the punch can be mastered. Dragon energy flow is extenuated in three steps:

- Heel to knee
- Knee to hip
- Waist to head

The elemental aspects of punching will be taught to coincide with the natural energy flow of movement. Taught are the 5 element theories of metal, wood, water, fire and earth. These elements are taught in both the outward external and the inward internal training theories of Pai Lum Tao.

Although filled with a seemingly endless arsenal of punches and strikes in Pai Lum Tao, a student's journey begins by trying to master four basic hand training skills:

1. Gong—Hard (Strength of a diamond)
2. Yuen—Soft (Razor sharp blade)
3. Jow—Claw (Spirit of the animal)
4. Lotus hand—Inward (Expel chi at will)

Found within the basics are a variation of theories. Such variations are apparent in the first punch taught—the reverse ram's head punch.

Contemporary way—The punch chambers at the waist. The punch is thrown to the target beginning with the fore knuckles facing down and twisting just prior to impact to the fore knuckles facing up.

Ancient way—The twisting of the fist begins just as it leaves the waist and fore knuckles travel up to the target. Such diversity is common in Pai Lum Tao.

The term "punch" may mislead some to believe that the hand must be closed tightly to strike. All parts of the hand will be used to strike carefully calculated targets. Such areas of the hand include:

- Two-knuckle
- Four-knuckle
- Fingertips
- Inside ridge
- Back knuckle
- Outside blade (chop)
- Heel palm
- Full palm

These make up the basic areas used in combat. The time-tested winning formula combining proper stance, aligned posture, timed energy flow, harmonic breathing, instinctive foresight, disciplined visualization, keen focus and precise execution make Pai Lum Tao's devastating punches a standard by which to be judged.

"The best punch in the world is no good, if it missed its target."

—Si Tai Gung Glenn C. Wilson

BACK KNUCKLE

BANDIT'S HEAD

BUTTERFLY PALMS

CRAB CLAW

DRAGON'S HEAD

EYE OF THE PHOENIX

FANNING CLOUDS

HAMMER FIST

IMMORTAL MAN POINTS THE WAY

KNIFE HANDS

LEOPARD PAW

LONG HAND

PRAYING MANTIS

REVERSE RAM'S HEAD

SHORT HAND

SUN FIST

TIGER CLAW

TWIN DRAGON SEARCHING FOR PEARLS

WHITE SNAKE HEAD

INSIDE WING

OUTSIDE WING

Kicks

With perfectly good hand techniques, why would anyone want to kick? Because to know the thunderous kicks of Pai Lum Tao is to understand the root strength of a great oak.

Kicks maintain an advantage over punches with their fundamental differences. Kicks may be executed close in or far away and they maintain a greater amount of mass and power. The legwork practiced in Pai Lum Tao is known as the drills of "leg fighting" (T'io tou ou). The legs serve as a battering ram, checkpoint, trapping tool and fulcrum from which to execute further techniques.

Such key factors as power, speed, conditioning and deliverance are the ingredients for success. Pai Lum Tao kicks are used to lead the barrage, break down the root, dislodge weight distribution, intercept assaulting techniques, trap and disorientate, as well as finish a confrontation with crushing and slicing techniques that penetrate and cut through the attack.

Kicks should be delivered with extreme power and execution to penetrate pinpoint target areas. Power kicks instruction begins with hours of slow, disciplined kick execution. Kicks are performed in an easy, isometric fashion until the muscles, tendons and ligaments have been properly conditioned. When this is accomplished, you begin to develop power with "the bag". This entails drilling first with the sawdust bag and later a sandbag. The power developed through sandbag training is incredible, so much so it is not uncommon for a Pai Lum Tao practitioner to shatter the leg of a wooden dummy in half with a shin strike.

Some of the basic standards for kicking include:
- Never leaving the groin exposed;
- Shifting weight to the supporting leg prior to the kick;

- Exhaling when kicking, matching the breath with the kick;
- Aiming kicks from the waist down;
- Kicking to, into, then through the targeted area;
- Relaxing the body for maximum Chi flow;
- Dragon waist whipping for maximum penetration and power;
- Keeping the supporting leg "foot" flat on the ground;
- Quickly retracting to the original position;
- Chopping the opponent's base or foundation; and
- Mastering the concept of whipping and snapping.

The speed of your kick goes hand in hand with timing and targetry. Speed is maximized by practicing basic drills, including thousands of kicks in front of a mirror partner. The more you practice, the more your kicks become relaxed extensions of your body. This modern form of training has proven its worth many times over. Kicking speed can only be mastered when the body is totally relaxed. Proper breathing patterns must be practiced to relieve the body of stress, tension and stiffening. The kick should explode from a set position to full speed with maximum penetration in the blink of an eye.

Speed drills include:
- Teasing the butterfly
- Snapping the whip
- Leg swing—Pendulum series
- Feather sequence
- Quick draw

Conditioning the legs helps a practitioner execute power penetration-type kicks without fear of injury. The formula for leg conditioning is:
- Seven star partner drills
- Wooden leg training
- Cane striking drills

- Sandbag drills
- Wooden post drills
- Iron pole sets
- Stone bag sets

These drills and sets lead to a mastery of Iron Leg techniques, which have been called some of the fastest and most powerful in any martial arts arsenal. When you understand the philosophy behind removing the foundation, the importance of conditioning in Pai Lum Tao training becomes readily apparent.

Powerful leg blocks, checks and traps also are a byproduct of such rigorous training. Basic Pai Lum Tao leg fighting techniques include:

- Ax Chopping Kick
- Back Thrust
- Inside Crescent Moon
- Outside Crescent Moon
- Front Snap Kick
- Front Stomp Kick
- Hook Kick
- Knife Edge Kick
- Rising Earth
- Rising Star
- Roundhouse Kick
- Scooping Monk Spade
- Side Thrust Kick
- Wheel Turning Kick

AX CHOPPING KICK

BACK THRUST

INSIDE CRESCENT MOON

OUTSIDE CRESCENT MOON

FRONT SNAP KICK

FRONT STOMP KICK

HOOK KICK

KNIFE EDGE KICK

RISING EARTH

RISING STAR

ROUNDHOUSE KICK

SCOOPING MONK'S SPADE

SIDE THRUST KICK

WHEEL TURNING KICK

Five Animal Styles

The five animals are dragon, tiger, leopard, snake and crane. According to ancient manuscripts, each animal has a distinct and accompanying action. Man has five essences: spirit, bone, strength, chi and sinew. These essences must be merged into one. It is important these essences include the basis of hard and soft movements and the translation of Gong-Yuen. No fighter can be truly powerful until all 170 actions and five essences work in harmony.

THE DRAGON

The dragon style represents the cultivation of spirit and wisdom; in short, the philosophy of the art of kung-fu. Strength is used through chi and the power of the mind. Any strike or kick should move naturally. Speed will result as the body relaxes and the mind is clear of other thoughts. The white dragon is all powerful and can change shape and form at will to facilitate victory.

THE TIGER

The tiger style represents the training of the bones. Brace yourself and practice firmly. Hand conditioning and solid body exercises represent the strength and ferocity of the tiger.

THE LEOPARD

The leopard style is one of power and explosiveness. The leopard springs at its adversary with lightning speed, subduing the attacker with powerful paw punches and claws.

THE SNAKE

The snake style represents rhythmic endurance and cultivation of chi. In the snake, you must move swiftly but remain low to the ground to draw strength from the earth. The movement of the hand should resemble the deadly strike of the cobra.

THE CRANE

The crane style represents gracefulness, balance, and sinew changing. All movements are in balance and harmony.

forms

Forms are the long stories of which wars are made. These are the stories that tell of victory and survival. With exact rhythm the stances, blocks, punches and kicks are played in an orchestrated fashion. At the end of a victorious encounter, the Pai Lum Tao warrior always displays a salute of remorse.

Low, powerful stances, coupled with evasive footwork, deceptive hand routines and lightning-fast explosive hand techniques, are a Pai Lum Tao student's formula for success.

Forms will teach balance, iron power legs, articulate timing, enhanced chi flow, rapid-fire punches, animalistic rhythm, and a feeling of honor and self-pride.

WHITE DRAGON WARRIOR SOCIETY
TRAINING FORMS
GRANDMASTER GLENN C. WILSON

Short Hand

Short Form of the Tiger

Movement of the Tiger

Twist of the Tiger

Hung Form 1 & 2

Outer Tiger

Inner Tiger

Flowing Seas

Eight Trigrams

Finger Set

Box Set

Five Animal Short Form

Chinese Soft Fist

Thousand Step

Mighty Wings of the Eagle

Dragon Dance

Short Dragon Set

Golden Fist

Hun 1-3

Pai Will

Wooden Dummy

White Dragon Fist Law

Elbow Sequence

Long Hand

Blocking the Line 1-4

Fast Accurate Fist

18 Hands of Lo Han

Plum Flower 1-3

Pai Lum 1-3

Tiger Goes Hunting

White Crane 1-3

Dragon Plays with 7 Stars

Flowing Motion 1 & 2

Pa Kow

Ling Po

Prance of the Panther

Northern Long Fist 1-3

Black Tiger 1 & 2

Lung Huit

Lo Han #1-7

Tiger Plays

Cat Plays

10 Creature Form

Monkey 1-3

Internal Hand

Kuan Yin Chi Kung 1-8

Yang Short Form

Yang Long Form 1-6

5 Element Form

Ghost Walking Form

Water Form

Penetrate the Wind

Pai Chi 1 & 2

Plum Blossom Chi

Tai Pai Lung Chi Long Form

Line Blocking Two

Silent Dragon

Dragon Prepare Leave Cave

Four Winds

Plum Section

Dragon Walks the Box

Chakra Set

Iron Ring

Weapons

Saber

Staff Set 1-3

Double Axes

Double Gim

Halberd

Horse Cutter

Two-Sectional Staff

Katana Battle Set

Katana 7 Ways of Cutting

Spear

Hook Swords

Double Sticks

Flute

Double-Headed Spear 1-2

Steel Whip

Ring Knives

Kwan Dao

Gim

Three-Sectional Staff 1-2

Butterfly Knives

Double Saber

Yuen Chuan Sequence

SHORT FORM OF THE TIGER
PAI LUM TAO'S 1ST "SHORT HAND" FORM

As with all Pai Lum Tao forms, a story is being told. The practitioner takes on the characteristics of the powerful tiger. The tiger meets its 11 attackers, yielding no ground. The virtues of tiger are practiced in this short form as well as the continuation forms called movements of the tiger and twist of the tiger. These three short-hand forms set a strong foundation for the Pai Lum Tao practitioner.

Tiger-style training develops rock-solid arms by training close to the bone. It features firm, powerful stances, coupled with fierce intensity at the time of execution. Power and a keen foresight are the balance of nature for the mighty tiger.

1–3. From ready stance, step to the right into a rooted square horse stance with an upward crane crossing wings gong chuan.

4. Execute a downward twin hammer strike to the side.

5. Continuing the energy, circle the arms in, up and out to strike with twin sun fists to the high zone. Reset with bent wings.

6. Look to the right then adjust the right foot. Turn to the right and execute a windmill block, left then right. You should be standing in a shallow long bow.

7. Your hands flow through a chamber into an iron butterfly at the high zone. You are in a crouching stance.

8. Lock and row the hands into the body and out to a 135-degree position to the left. The stance drops into a rooted side horse stance.

9. Your hands turn into tiger claws. Then, with tension, rip out, short with the left and long with the right.

10

10. Lean only the upper body to the left. At the same time, execute a left palm strike and right arm post to the attacking limb.

11–12. Slip a left tiger claw under the right arm. Clear the right arm with the left tiger claw while stepping back into a ready stance with the left tiger claw in front of body.

11

12

13–15. Circle the left wing out and execute an outward white crane wing strike. Pause for a second, then execute a reverse elbow strike into the chambered hand.

13

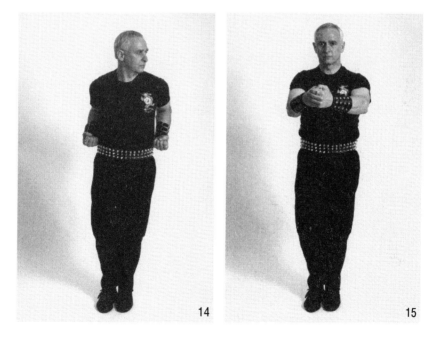

14

15

SELF-DEFENSE FIST SETS

"Battles are made of 'fists sets,' Wars are made of 'forms.'"

—Professor—Glenn C. Wilson
(Bok Leen Pai)

All fist sets tell a short story through its intricate movements. These smooth, fluid, powerful sets depict the very essence of Pai Lum Tao—its ability to defend and protect.

A student will study these traditional short stories of battles while still working his forms, alternate patterns, and chi development. The objective is total peace. There are 74 self-defense fist sets between a White sash/belt novice and the honored student testing for his Black sash/belt Level One. The fist sets will challenge your endurance, pinpoint targetry, power, rhythm, speed, foresight and total understanding of the system we call "Pai Lum Tao".

Beginner fist sets are taught in this order:

- Yielding Fire
- Bite of the Viper
- Removing the Jewels
- Hidden Spear
- Escaping Sparrow
- Pushing the Circle
- Thunder and Earth
- Penetrating Earth
- Dangerous Waters
- Gentle Thunder
- Twisting Bird
- Tiger in the Cave
- Arousing Mountain
- Tackle Techniques
- Sumo
- Crash of the Eagle
- Rising Elbow
- Opponent at Sides
- Passing the Horizon
- Wrap-arounds
- Kimono Grab
- Lever

YIELDING FIRE
Attack: Bear Hug From Behind

- As your right hand holds the attacker's grab, step out with the right foot. This pulls the attacker off balance.
- "V-step" with the left foot behind the attacker's right foot.
- Execute a left elbow to the solar plexus, left hammer fist to the groin, and left twin dragon's searching for the pearls to the right eye.

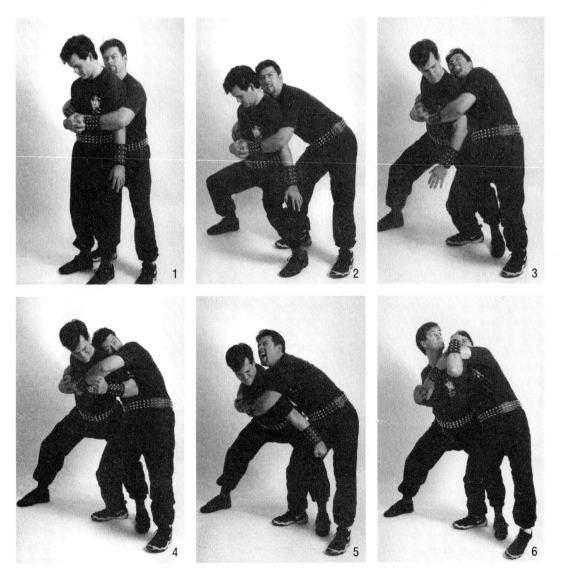

BITE OF THE VIPER
Attack: Front Snap Kick

- Assume a side horse stance with the left leg back. Use a cross-arm gong chuan block over the front leg with the right arm on top.
- Apply a right sun fist to the ribs.
- And a right leopard's paw (fingers up) to the throat. Maintain a gong chuan guard with the left hand.

REMOVING THE JEWELS
Attack: Headlock on your left side.

- Left uppercut to the ribs.
- Right tiger's claw to the groin. Left hand chambered at the right shoulder. Long bow stance.
- Transition to right back setting tiger as you extract "the jewels" and slap the groin with your left hand. Your right hand is at a 45-degree angle after the extraction. Apply a back noni slap to the groin.

HIDDEN SPEAR
Attack: The attacker's left arm is on your left shoulder from behind.

- Step with right foot to the left 45 degrees.
- Double spears (snake hands) come up as you pivot left into a cat stance, hitting the attacker's arms. Be sure your arms are at a 45-degree angle so you can intersect the attacker.
- Grab his left arm with your left hand, twist so the elbow is pointed up, and execute a left-side heel kick to the ribs.
- Chamber your left foot in front of your right to a monkey stance, maintaining a grip on the wrist until the attacker is off balance. Execute a tiger claw down into the attacker's head as you pull him into you.

ESCAPING SPARROW

Attack: Attacker grabs your right wrist with his right hand.

- Step left with your left foot.
- Your right hand crosses in front and forms a crane's beak as it circles to trap the attacker's wrist.
- Follow with a left crane's head punch to the attacker's head.
- You will end up in a right long bow stance. When the right arm comes around you may find that the attacker will trip over your leg.

PUSHING THE CIRCLE
Attack: Right wrist grabbed by left hand.

- Step right on the 45.
- Push the attacker's arm forward, tracing a counterclockwise circle.
- Re-enforce the right elbow into the attacker's exposed rib cage. Side horse stance.

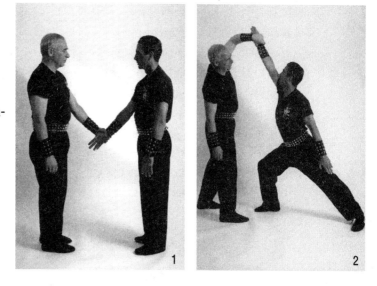

- Use a reverse outside wing punch to the upper zone. Chamber at the left shoulder.
- Use a reverse outside wing to the groin.

THUNDER AND EARTH
Attack: Double Lapel Grab

- Hands go up between the attacker's arms (yuen chuan with palms facing you). They clear the grab and set at a 45-degree angle. Lift your right leg up into a crane stance.
- Right front snap kick to the groin.
- Set down on his right leg and follow with a right inside gong chuan block to the wrist. Add a left willow palm to the elbow.
- Step forward with the right leg, press with the left willow palm and execute a right hammer fist to the collarbone.
- Open your right hand, step forward with the right leg and execute a left elbow to the head.

PENETRATING EARTH
Attack: Arm bar (Hammerlock) on your right arm.

- Grab your attacker's right wrist with your right hand (behind your back).
- Step right, dislodging the weight.
- Left elbow strike to the attacker's rib cage.
- Add a left stomp to the attacker's left foot.
- With the left foot step northeast at a 45-degree angle.
- Rotate on the heel of your left foot and ball of the right foot to side horse stance. This will pull your attacker further off balance.
- Your left arm traps the attacker's right arm with the monkey's paw, allowing your right arm to break free.
- Strike the attacker mid-zone with a right ram's head and high zone with a right sun fist.

DANGEROUS WATERS
Attack: Front grab to your left wrist.

- Chamber your right hand yuen chuan at shoulder level.
- Come down with your arm and strike the attacker's wrist.
  Note: The point of the attack should be the nerve endings at the wrist. This will stun the attacker.
- At the same time pull your left hand free, chamber at the left shoulder, and execute an iron fan to attacker's eyes. Your right arm remains extended as a guard.

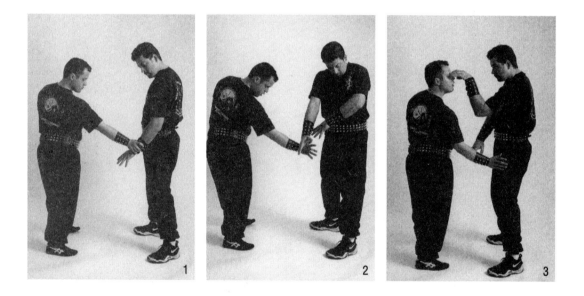

GENTLE THUNDER
Attack: Shoulder grab from behind.

- Left stomp to the attacker's left foot.
- Extend the left arm out yuen chuan between your waist and knee and stomp with the right foot to northwest 45 degrees. Twist the foot to get maximum rotation.
- Pivot on the right ball and left heel, bringing the left arm over at a 45-degree angle and striking the attacker's arm.
- Set in long bow, strike with right reverse ram.

TWISTING BIRD
Attack: Single lapel grab.

- Step back with your left foot to a side horse stance.
- As your left hand guards your rib cage, your right arm circles clockwise, breaking the attacker's grab and arm with the elbow. The hand is open in yuen chuan.
- Pivot on your right toe, pointing the knee to the ground (the bird twists). Strike the throat with a right leopard's paw, palm up.

TIGER IN THE CAVE
Attack: Bear hug from behind—Your arms are free.

- Step left, strike the attacker's hands with your knuckles to stun him and butt strike at the same time.
- Left re-enforce elbow strike to the attacker's face.
- Right re-enforce elbow strike to the attacker's face.
- Shift (hop) to a southwest 45-degree

long bow. Left outside wing to the attacker's neck. Right willow palm guard at your solar plexus. On the pivot your right leg will sweep the attacker's right leg.

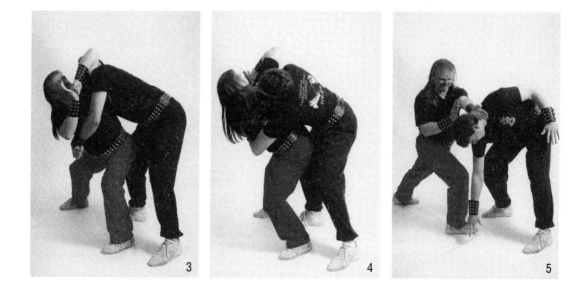

AROUSING MOUNTAIN
Attack: Punch to the face.

- Step back with the right foot.
- The left hand clears in front of the face and continues around to form the short wing. Reinforce with the right.
- Shuffle forward and left elbow strike to the attacker's ribs. Assume a side horse stance.
- Left hammer fist to the groin. Pivot to short bow.
- Long bow right reverse ram.

Tackle Techniques
Attack: Attacker lunges at you from the front.

- Step back into a side horse.
- A left yuen chuan clears through and chambers in front of your forehead, palm out.
- Apply a right outside wing punch to the medulla area of the attacker's head.

SUMO
Attack: Double grab midsection.

- Step out left as both arms come up overhead. Palms facing you, with the left closest to you. Set in a squatted stance. Your elbows come down and break the attacker's grip.
- Strike to the throat.
- Right foot light leg stepping forward. Right elbow is under the attacker's chin.
- Pivot and strike with a right upper hammer to the groin.
- Right back kick.
- The right leg crosses in front of the left leg and sets.
- Double yuen chuan guards to the rear (pointing to the attacker).
- Pivot right heel left ball to a side horse stance, right-left windmill guard.

CRASH OF THE EAGLE
Attack: Double choke from behind.

- Left foot forward.
- Start with a right downward elbow strike to the attacker's arm. Hand is open and closes to gong chuan as it comes down.
- Execute the following: Upward elbow to the chin, back knuckle to the face, eagle claw to the face, inside wing, outside wing, reverse bow stance and hammer fist—groin, back kick to the chest.

RISING ELBOW
Attack: Bear hug arms pinned.

- Right foot to square horse.
- Left hammer fist to the groin. Left leg steps behind. Change to tiger claw and grab the groin. Extract the groin as the elbow rises under the attacker's chin.

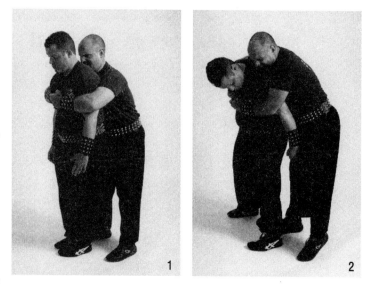

- The attacker is now bent over your left leg. Right hammer to the groin. Move to a right twisted horse stance, knee down.

OPPONENT AT SIDES
Attack: Two attackers—one on each side.
Hand on your shoulder.

- Left hand on attacker's hand. Step right to a horse stance. Right reverse outside wing to the throat.
- Cross-step right in front, placing your foot behind the attacker's left, if possible.
- The left hand clears away the arm of the attacker on your left side.
- Pivot. Right outside wing. Left hand ends with the palm facing you.

PASSING THE HORIZON
Attack: Right arm bar from behind.

- Regrab the attacker's wrist and step back with the left foot, striking the chin with your left elbow. Assume a side horse stance.
- Your left leg steps forward to 12 o'clock. Pivot around and grab the attacker's hand. You now have both hands on his wrist. Turn his arm (wristlock) to expose the elbow.
- Step back with the right leg and extend the attacker's body.
- Right front snap kick to the face.

WRAP-AROUNDS
Attack: Shoulder grab from the side.

- No steps!
- Look at the attacker. Pin hand to your shoulder.
- Your elbow circles up and comes down to break the attacker's arm. The fist strikes with the back knuckle.
- Finish with a sun fist to the face.

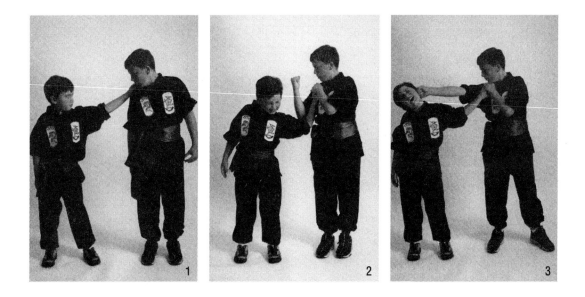

KIMONO GRAB
Attack: Two-handed grab to the lapels.

- Your left hand goes over the right hand of the attacker and grabs his left wrist. Bring your left elbow to your chest and trap the attacker's arm. This will pull him off balance.
- Step back with the left foot to long bow and execute a right spearhand between the attacker's arms to the throat.
- Transition to a square horse as you circle the right hand, gong chuan, to the outside. Come down to break the arms of the attacker. Execute an outside wing to the throat.
- Shuffle step and execute a reinforced right elbow to the face, pivot on the right foot, execute a hammer fist to the groin, back kick to the groin, step out and set.

LEVER
Attack: Left grab right chest.

- Grab the arm and step back with the left leg.
- Right reverse outside wing to break the elbow.
- Rake down the arm to burn the nerves. At this point release the attacker's arm.
- Reverse outside wing to the throat.

Pai Lum Tao Terminology

Founder/Great Grandmaster _____ Si Jo
Grandmaster _____ Si Tai Gung
Senior Master _____ 8th Higher Level and up
Professor _____ 6th Higher Level and up
Master_____ Si Gung, 4th Higher Level and up
Instructor _____ Si Fu
Senior student (not a full teacher)_____ Si Hing
Wife of a Head Master (may also be a Si Fu) _____ Si Mo
School _____ Kwoon
Ceremonial Bow_____ I Shih Chu Kung
Uniform _____ Sahm
Meditation_____ Chung Tsai
Kick _____ Tsu
Punch _____ Ta
Block _____ Feng So
Stance _____ Li Tsu Ti
Hard _____ Gong
Soft_____ Yuen
Fist _____ Chuan
The Way_____ Tao
White _____ Pai/Bai
Dragon _____ Lum/Lung
Martial Art _____ Kuo Shu

Beginner's Program

Sit_____ Sto
Neck circles _____ Ching pu huan
Back stretch (leg out)_____ Pei pu shen chang
Shoulder rotations_____ Chien hsuan chuan

Head to knee (inhale, down, up, exhale;
count moving hands and toes) _ _ _ _ _ _ _ _ _ _ _ T'ou hsing hsi
Back stretch_ _ _ _ _ _ _ _ _ _ _ _ _ _ _ _ _ _ _ Pei pu shen chang
Leg split _ T'ui fen lieh
Head to floor _ _ _ _ _ _ _ _ _ _ _ _ _ _ _ _ _ T'ou hsiang ti pan
Head to knee and alternate _ _ _ _ _ _ _ T'ou shiang hsi, lun liu
Sit-ups _ Tso tsai shang
Stand up to kneeling _ _ _ _ _ _ _ _ _ _ _ _ _ _ _ _ _ Chan ch'i
Side leg stretch_ _ _ _ _ _ _ _ _ _ _ _ _ _ Pien t'ui shen chang
Head to knee _ _ _ _ _ _ _ _ _ _ _ _ _ _ _ _ _ _ T'ou hsing hsi
Front split_ _ _ _ _ _ _ _ _ _ _ _ _ _ _ _ Ch'ien mien fen lieh
Leg lift (two people) Front, Side, Back _ _ _ _ _ _ _ _ T'ui chu chi

Basics—Chi ch'u te
Kicks _ _ _ _ _ _ _ _ _ _ _ _ _ _ Ts'u (position, rapid breathing)
Front snap kick _ _ _ _ _ _ _ _ _ _ _ _ _ Chein mien chi jui sheng
Sidekick _ Pien ts'u
Back kick _ _ _ _ _ _ _ _ _ _ _ _ _ _ _ _ _ _ Tsai oh mien te ts'u
Roundkick _ _ _ _ _ _ _ _ _ _ _ _ _ _ A yuan te fang wu ts'u
Hook kick _ Kou ts'u
Jump kick _ _ _ _ _ _ _ _ _ _ _ _ _ _ _ _ _ _ _ T'iao yush ts'u
Crescent kick _ _ _ _ _ _ _ _ _ _ _ _ _ _ _ _ _ _ Hsin yueh ts'u

Stances—Li tsu ti
Lunge_ Ch'ien chin te
Horse_ Ma
Break stance_ _ _ _ _ _ _ _ _ _ _ _ _ _ _ _ Chung ch'ang te
Monkey _ Hou
Bow and arrow_ _ _ _ _ _ _ _ _ _ _ _ _ _ _ _ _ _ Kung shih
Cat_ Mao
Twisted_ Niu chuan
Hour glass _ _ _ _ _ _ _ _ _ _ _ _ _ _ _ _ _ Chih chien po li

Strikes—Ta

Front punch _ Chien mien ch'uan ta
Hook punch _ Kou chu'an ta
Backfist _ Tsai hou mien te ta
Uppercut _ Tsai shang te ta

Blocks—Feng so

Upper _ _ _ _ _ _ _ _ _ _ _ _ _ _ _ _ _ _ _ Hsiang shang ta feng so
Inside _ Nie pu wu feng so
Outside_ _ _ _ _ _ _ _ _ _ _ _ _ _ _ _ _ _ _ Wai pu te feng so
Lower _ _ _ _ _ _ _ _ _ _ _ _ _ _ _ _ _ _ Shaing shia te feng so
Circle _ _ _ _ _ _ _ _ _ _ _ _ _ _ _ _ _ _ _ Yuan te feng so

Self-defense—Tsu fang yu

Monkey grab _ Hou shin wo
Spider walk _ _ _ _ _ _ _ _ _ _ _ _ _ _ _ _ _ _ _ Chih chu san pu
Five star _ Wu hsing

Fighting forms—Tou ou hsing chuang

Monkey grab (Inside/Outside) _ _ Hou shin wo nei pu te wai pu te
Palm block and grab _ _ _ _ _ _ Shou chang feng so chi chin wa
Five star (One-side attack, one-side block)_ _ _ _ _ _ _ Wu-hsing
Freestyle _ _ _ _ _ _ _ _ _ _ _ _ _ _ _ _ Tzu yu te shih yang tou ou

Chinese Numbers

One (1)_ _ _ _ _ _ _ _ _ _ Ee
Two (2) _ _ _ _ _ _ _ _ _ _ Er
Three (3)_ _ _ _ _ _ _ _ _ San
Four (4) _ _ _ _ _ _ _ _ _ Su
Five (5)_ _ _ _ _ _ _ _ _ _ Wu

Six (6) _ _ _ _ _ _ _ _ _ _ _ Leiu
Seven (7) _ _ _ _ _ _ _ _ _ _ Chi
Eight (8)_ _ _ _ _ _ _ _ _ _ _ Pa
Nine (9) _ _ _ _ _ _ _ _ _ Chew
Ten (10) _ _ _ _ _ _ _ _ _ Shih

Pai Lum Tao Tree

(As told to disciple Glenn C. Wilson in Orlando, Fla., in 1992 by Dr. Daniel Kane Pai

Pai Te Lung Chuan Kung-Fu • Bok Leen Pai Kenpo • Pai Yung Tai Chi Chuan

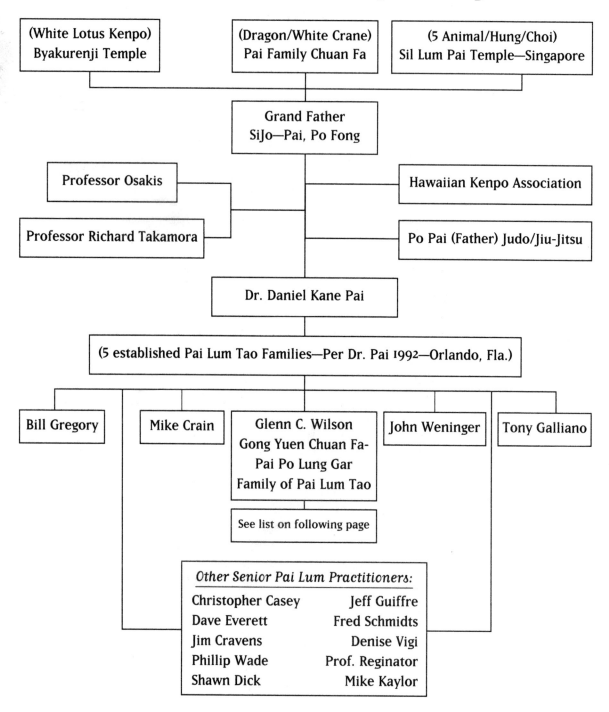

(White Lotus Kenpo) Byakurenji Temple	(Dragon/White Crane) Pai Family Chuan Fa	(5 Animal/Hung/Choi) Sil Lum Pai Temple—Singapore

Grand Father
SiJo—Pai, Po Fong

Professor Osakis	Hawaiian Kenpo Association
Professor Richard Takamora	Po Pai (Father) Judo/Jiu-Jitsu

Dr. Daniel Kane Pai

(5 established Pai Lum Tao Families—Per Dr. Pai 1992—Orlando, Fla.)

Bill Gregory	Mike Crain	Glenn C. Wilson Gong Yuen Chuan Fa- Pai Po Lung Gar Family of Pai Lum Tao	John Weninger	Tony Galliano

See list on following page

Other Senior Pai Lum Practitioners:

Christopher Casey	Jeff Guiffre
Dave Everett	Fred Schmidts
Jim Cravens	Denise Vigi
Phillip Wade	Prof. Reginator
Shawn Dick	Mike Kaylor

Gong Yuen Chuan Fa Family

(Instructors)

Glenn C. Wilson	Randy Sharkey
Rusty Gray	Conrad Blasko
Bobby Earl	Steve Jungman
John Springer	Chuck Burnett
Ashley King	Keith Fain
Don Wilson	Larry Thornhill
Laura Middaugh	Jeff Sindy
Bruce Gates	Cynthia Rothrock
Rick Sharlou	Steve Wallace
Michael Candeloro	Oscar Long
Michael Broshire	Bill Sciano
Bob Stauble	Martin Rodriquez
Jeff Hosie	James Hickey
Bob Wallace	Bill McAllife
Dave Lewis	Eric La Cuyer
Brian Felter	Doug Ford
Hilda Wilson	Kenny Brown
James Wilson	Carlos Aguilar
Larry Greene	Fred Satterfield
Bill Frost	Kyle Perry
Jimmy Wilson	Rich Wilson
Ron Caimano	Milton Rivera
Rick Armstrong	Al Villacampa
Barry Hallman	Burrie Pinnex
Joe McGuire	Patrick Finneran
Gus Marquardt	Robert Murphy
Bill Hunter	Paul West
Lora Damiani	Luis Felix
Tam Nguyen	Rich McKay
Umar Arrastia	Paul Conforti
Janet Emken	Rich Boki

Conclusion

In the search of your study you must keep in mind the following concerns. One searches to know his greater self and a higher level of awareness with the affairs of the world. The situations of the past, present and future develop our character and nature. You cannot change the nature of the beast; only alter its behavior for a short time. The secrets of our discipline lie within our movement. Your chi will develop through the marriage of movement and interaction of body, mind and spirit.

Fulfillment lies within your true nature. We strive for balance within us. The philosophies of Pai Lum Tao teach us to strive to exist at the center of nature—to discover the middle path.

Those who take the initiative to master the "Way of the White Dragon" will walk the middle path, find the center of their own nature, diminish ego, and find peace and direction through the discipline of their training.

Pai Lum Tao teaches the unity of mind, body and spirit. It seeks a balance as depicted by the unity of yin/yang, while always remembering "survival of the fittest" remains an important consideration.

I hope these writings will help peoples' lives and assist in spreading a positive energy. Practice the Shaolin Chuan Fa saying "Dragon's Creed"—Seek Peace Always, But if the Soul is Threatened, Let the Soul Become Warrior.

"In the spirit of the White Dragon"

—Grandmaster—Professor, Glenn C. Wilson